The Other Side of Addiction Letters to an Addict

SARA HEAVILIN

BookLeaf Publishing

India | USA | UK

Presentation by *BookLeaf Publishing*

Web: www.bookleafpub.com

E-mail: info@bookleafpub.com

ISBN: 9789358735154

First edition 2023

Fences

I built a fence
I used to peer through
The slats
Now the weeds have
Taken over
Litter strewn about
In the growth
It saddens me to see
such beauty
Overrun by neglect
Abused by a mind
That allows others to litter
Such waste and hate
On such a beautiful soul
I still see a person
That resembles you
I built a fence
I no longer peer through
The slats
To watch someone
I no longer know
On repeat

Empty Bottles

An empty bottle of wine
An empty bottle of pills
Black cat perched on her back
Everything neatly put away
Gray ash in the cold fireplace
The dog licks her hand
The cat jumps to the floor
An empty bottle of wine
An empty bottle of pills
My heart continues
To beat
Yours stopped
My world now a little emptier
All for an empty bottle of wine
And an empty bottle of pills.

Lessons In Loving An Addict

No junior prom
No senior prom
No graduation
I watched other people
Posting their photos
I swept it away
Like it didn't really matter
Did it?
You were fighting ghosts
I was juggling life
Learning how to love you
Watching your hand
Slip from mine
As you slid into
The abyss
Then none of it mattered
It became a game of
Are you still alive
And I couldn't breathe
Message read
Air in my lungs
Still alive
You taught me to
Live for the moment
Just day by day

You were my lesson
In learning
To love an addict

Meant To Be

5

You are exactly where You are meant to be
That's what I tell myself daily
That means that you are also
Exactly where you are meant to be
And I don't understand
How anyone is meant to be
Addicted to a substance

Angry

I'm not angry
Anger is a secondary emotion
So I'm not angry
I'm sad
I'm not angry
I'm scared
I'm not angry
I'm frustrated
I am many things
Anger doesn't get to
Reside inside any more
Letting go
I've done a lot of that
Sadness is a much lighter
Burden to carry
Because I've learned
That I can be happy
Even when there are
Things that make me sad
That I can still live
And be alive
While mourning

Denial

I watched in silent denial
The very idea absurd
It isn't that bad
It isn't possible

Loving An Addict

And the hardest thing to accept is that you
Lost to a substance, a feeling of needing to chase
a rush.
And that chase is more important than anything
else.
And that trying to hold onto a person that no
longer exists is killing you.
And the tighter you grasp,
the harder it is to breathe.
Your throat raw
Your hands hurt.
Your heart, crushed.
You're certain there is a rip somewhere Every
piece of you that matters is escaping.
You know it isn't yours.
You learn to accept that you lost to a substance.
You lost to a rush, a high that you can't compete
with.
You lost someone, but they are still alive.
Breathing, living, laughing, alive.
But not really living.
And the grip you have loosens.
And then you let go.
Your throat still raw.
Your hands cut deep.

Your heart broken, you begin the work
Of loving someone you don't even know.
You learn to walk without them.
And you accept that this is the way it is.
And you realize you'd already learned to live
without them.
This is loving an addict.

The List

You make a list
Of all that is wrong with me
I know that's not who I am
So I do my best to be
This person you think
I should be
The list keeps growing
Just like the bottles
On the counter
As they empty
One by one
The list of my faults
Is added to
Until it was impossible
To attain
I've realized that just
Like those bottles
That list was never truly mine

Can't Hate You

I can't hate you
I have tried
I want to hate you
Some days
I want to yell
And scream
I want to make you understand
What you are doing
Kills me inside
The things you have
Said and done
That I didn't deserve
You choose a substance
And still I can't hate you

Loving You

It's a different kind of pain
Loving you
I feel it in my bones
A dull throbbing
I can't hate you
I still have to move forward
Pretending pieces don't shatter
Pretending it doesn't matter
I laugh while my heart rips
Dull throbbing
I feel it in my bones
While life keeps moving

Mirror

If I could find a mirror
to show you what I see.
You'd see that you're the scarecrow,
Smarter than you think.
You'd see that you're the lion,
Full of courage
You'd see that you're the tin man,
You always had the heart.
You'd see that you are Dorothy,
And you've always held the power.
If I could find that mirror
Maybe you'd believe.

Invitation Only

I no longer have a front row seat to watch the
destruction.
I don't even have lawn seats.
I walked away.
It's invitation only.
Mine was destroyed.
And all I can do is love you in silence.

Pretending

And what a life….
To have to pretend that everything is okay when
it isn't.
To live like a part of me
Isn't dying
To know what people
Must think
This is my life
Pretending that everything is okay
When it isn't

Ghosts

Have you ever seen a ghost, she asked
I've loved them, I replied
Loved them? She inquired
Not always side by side
Sometimes from a distance
While they battle their demons
Their silence more deafening
Than their cries and outbursts
And I haven't decided if their
Death would bring more peace
For me or them
Always hopeful they'll
Find their way home

Wishes

I Wish I Had….
Held you more, even when I was mad.
Kissed you more of the chances I had.
Told you your importance in my life.
Showed you when I was afraid
Say I needed your help.
I should have held you closer
Told you everything will be ok
Sing that song just one more time
BUT
I didn't do those things
I just thought you knew.
I would wade through hell
If it meant saving you
I wish I had told you
These things
BUT
I didn't
Wishing doesn't change this
I know this all too well
AND
Still I wish I had….

The Battle

Some days I feel stuck
Some days I forge ahead
Some days I'm seeped in sadness
But every day I try
To find happiness
Laughter
A smile
But really I'm a fake
A scammer
A fraud
Knowing everyone is right
I should just give up
Knowing everyone is wrong
I should never give up
Stuck in this battle
Between my heart and brain
Forging ahead to make my future
Heart broken
Barely breathing
Continuing on
Knowing I must

Demons

And the demons crawl in and through your
brain.
And you fight them every day.
The battles you fight no one
Knows anything about.
I loved those demons
Even when I lost
I love those demons
Even though I don't
Know them
They came with the package
That was you

Sacrifice

One is too many
Grant me the serenity
To accept
A thousand is never enough
The things I can't change
And I can't change you
So I had to have the courage
To accept and let go
Change the thing I could
Some call it wisdom
When you understand the difference
I call it a sacrifice
To save myself
Instead of saving you
Severing you nearly killed me
Staying would have
Meant wearing a mask
That would have suffocated me
Making me a living corpse
In your graveyard of bottles